Perseverance

OTHER BOOKS BY MARGARET J. WHEATLEY

Leadership and the New Science
A Simpler Way (with Myron Rogers)
Turning to One Another
Finding Our Way

PERSEVERANCE COVER ART - ASANTE SALAAM: Pressed flower petals, layers of packing tissue paper, charcoal, pencil, ink, the inside of a flattened cardboard box, and adhesive have been melded into this peaceful mixed media drawing. Repurposed materials collected in San Diego, Salaam's post-Katrina home, carry energy from previous use, while being reincarnated into a new creation. This untitled piece of transparent layers was formed through a meditative process incorporating visioning, sunlight, prayer, affirmations, fresh finger canyon breezes, and burgeoning faith.

Perseverance

MARGARET J. WHEATLEY

PAINTINGS BY ASANTE SALAAM

CALLIGRAPHY BY BARBARA BASH

BK

Berrett–Koehler Publishers, Inc.
San Francisco
a BK Life book

A BERKANA PUBLICATION

Berrett-Koehler Publishers, Inc.
235 Montgomery Street, Suite 650
San Francisco, CA 94104-2916
Tel: (415) 288-0260
Fax: (415) 362-2512
www.bkconnection.com

Ordering Information
Quantity sales. Special discounts are available on quantity purchases by corporations, associations, and others. For details, contact the "Special Sales Department" at the Berrett-Koehler address above.

Individual sales. Berrett-Koehler publications are available through most bookstores. They can also be ordered directly from Berrett-Koehler: Tel: (800) 929-2929; Fax: (802) 864-7626; www.bkconnection.com

Orders for college textbook/course adoption use. Please contact Berrett-Koehler: Tel: (800) 929-2929; Fax: (802) 864-7626.

Orders by U.S. trade bookstores and wholesalers. Please contact Ingram Publisher Services, Tel: (800) 509-4887; Fax: (800) 838-1149; E-mail: customer.service@ingrampublisherservices.com; or visit www.ingrampublisherservices.com/Ordering for details about electronic ordering.

Berrett-Koehler and the BK logo are registered trademarks of Berrett-Koehler Publishers, Inc.

Printed in the United States of America

Berrett-Koehler books are printed on long-lasting acid-free paper. When it is available, we choose paper that has been manufactured by environmentally responsible processes. These may include using trees grown in sustainable forests, incorporating recycled paper, minimizing chlorine in bleaching, or recycling the energy produced at the paper mill.

Library of Congress Cataloging-in-Publication Data

Wheatley, Margaret J.
Perseverance / by Margaret J. Wheatley.
p. cm.
ISBN 978-1-60509-820-3 (pbk. : alk. paper)
1. Perseverance (Ethics) I. Title.
BJ1533.P4W43 2010
179'.9--dc22
2010022949

First Edition
15 14 13 12   10 9 8 7 6 5 4

DEDICATION

For Free Floaters

I stand among you as one who
offers a small message of hope...
there are always people who dare
to seek on the margin of society,
who are not dependent
on social acceptance,
not dependent on social routine,
and prefer a kind of free-floating
existence under a state of risk.

Thomas Merton
Catholic monk, writer, activist

Contents

From the Elders of the Hopi Nation

ORAIBI, ARIZONA

TO MY FELLOW SWIMMERS:

Here is a river flowing now very fast.
It is so great and swift that there are those
who will be afraid, who will try
to hold on to the shore.
They are being torn apart and
will suffer greatly.

Know that the river has its destination.
The elders say we must let go of the shore.
Push off into the middle of the river,
and keep our heads above water.

And I say see who is there with you
and celebrate.
At this time in history,
we are to take nothing personally,
least of all ourselves,
for the moment we do,
our spiritual growth and journey come to a halt.

The time of the lone wolf is over.
Gather yourselves.
Banish the word struggle from your attitude
and vocabulary.

All that we do now must be done
in a sacred manner and in celebration.
For we are the ones we have been waiting for.

Questions and Answers

How is it that some people devote their lives to a cause, to a person, to a place?

And how is it that even in the midst of failures, betrayals, reversals, they can still remain focused and dedicated to their cause?

What enables a person to stay, to not be dissuaded, to not lose focus? How do people not become overwhelmed, or succumb to exhaustion and despair?

How do such people sustain themselves over long periods of time? How do they preserve their health and well-being?

How do they preserve their faith?

I want to be one who perseveres, so these are real questions for me.

I have been out in the world with these questions for many years now and met many people who have persevered through circumstances I hope never to encounter. I am grateful for all that I have learned from them—they answered many of my questions.

Of course there are many answers available. Here are just a few I discovered and found to be relevant in my own experience.

May the questions stay alive in your heart, and may these few answers serve you well so that you too may be one who perseveres.

Meg Wheatley

It is not necessary to hope in order to undertake,
nor to succeed in order to persevere.

Charles the Bold
Duke of Burgundy

Perseverance

The word "perseverance" in Latin means, "one who sees through to the end," "one who doesn't yield." In English, it describes how we maintain our activity in spite of difficulties. Tenacity, steadfastness, persistence, doggedness—these are all common synonyms.

In Chinese, the character for perseverance is often the same as the one used for patience.

Human experience is the story of perseverance. Throughout space and time, humans have always persevered. We wouldn't be here without them.

Think of all the people you know—family, friends, strangers—who have just kept going, who didn't yield, who were tenacious, steadfast, patient.

How would you describe them? What were some of their traits? Their capacities? What was it like to be around them, to listen to their stories?

At the end of their lives, how were they?

Angry? Contented? Cynical? Peaceful?

What do their lives offer you as lessons on how to persevere?

What do we all need to learn from them now?

A Knife

Here is the Chinese character for perseverance.
It is a knife poised over a heart.

Written in the ancient "seal style"

PART ONE

Here Is a River

TO MY FELLOW SWIMMERS:

Here is a river flowing now very fast.
It is so great and swift that there are those
who will be afraid, who will try
to hold on to the shore.
They are being torn apart and
will suffer greatly.

I'm making my shoulders strong
for the young to stand upon,
stepping lightly on the backs of those
who hold me up.
It's a chain of life unending,
ever new and ever bending,
grateful is the heart for the chance to be alive.

Susan Osborn
Singer/songwriter

We've Been Here Before

We have never been here before in terms of the global nature of our predicament. For the first time in human history (at least that we know of), we have endangered our home planet. And for the first time, we know what's happening to just about all 7 billion of us humans, the challenges and terrors we endure and the occasional, reaffirming triumphs. Never before have humans been so aware of one another's struggles, pain and perseverance. Never before have we known so many of the consequences of what we do—our thoughtless, violent, heroic and loving actions.

Yet we *have* been here before. In our long, mysterious history, humans have had to struggle with enormous upheavals, dislocations, famines and fears. We've had to counteract aggression, protect our loved ones and face the end of life as we've known it. Over and over again.

The scale is different now, but the human experience is the same. And so are our human spirits, capable of generosity or abuse, creativity or destruction, survival or extinction. As we face the challenges and struggles of this time, it might help to recall the centuries of solid shoulders we stand on.

And if you reflect on your own life experience, what else have you endured? You're still here—how did you stay here?

How have you come through rough times before?

What from your own personal history gives you now the capacity to get through this time?

What Time Is It?

It was the best of times, it was the worst of times,
it was the age of wisdom, it was the age of foolishness,
it was the epoch of belief, it was the epoch of incredulity,
it was the season of Light, it was the season of Darkness,
it was the spring of hope, it was the winter of despair,
we had everything before us, we had nothing before us,
we were all going direct to Heaven,
we were all going direct the other way.
In short, the period was so far like the present period,
that some of its noisiest authorities insisted
on its being received, for good or for evil,
in the superlative degree of comparison only.

Charles Dickens
A Tale of Two Cities, 1859

Ours is not the task of fixing the entire world
all at once, but of stretching out to mend the part
of the world that is within our reach. Any small,
calm thing that one soul can do to help another soul,
to assist some portion of this poor suffering world,
will help immensely.

Clarissa Pinkola Estes
Writer

It's Our Turn

Throughout human existence, there have always been people willing to step forward to struggle valiantly in the hope that they might reverse the downward course of events. Some succeeded, some did not. As we face our own time, it's good to remember that we're only the most recent humans who have struggled to change things.

Getting engaged in changing things is quite straightforward. If we have an idea, or want to resolve an injustice, or stop a tragedy, we step forward to serve. Instead of being overwhelmed and withdrawing, we act.

No grand actions are required; we just need to begin speaking up about what we care about. We don't need to spend a lot of time planning or getting senior leaders involved; we don't have to wait for official support. We just need to get started—for whatever issue or person we care about.

When we fail, which of course we often will, we don't have to feel discouraged. Instead, we can look into our mistakes and failures for the valuable learnings they contain. And we can be open to opportunities and help that present themselves, even when they're different from what we thought we needed. We can follow the energy of "Yes!" rather than accepting defeat or getting stuck in a plan.

This is how the world always changes. Everyday people not waiting for someone else to fix things or come to their rescue, but simply stepping forward, working together, figuring out how to make things better.

Now it's our turn.

The future is no more uncertain than the present.

Walt Whitman
Poet

Dwelling in Uncertainty

Some people despair about the darkening direction of the world today. Others are excited by the possibilities for creativity and new ways of living they see emerging out of the darkness.

Rather than thinking one perspective is preferable to the other, let's notice that both are somewhat dangerous. Either position, optimism or pessimism, keeps us from fully engaging with the complexity of this time. If we see only troubles, or only opportunities, in both cases we are blinded by our need for certainty, our need to know what's going on, to figure things out so we can be useful.

Certainty is a very effective way of defending ourselves from the irresolvable nature of life. If we're certain, we don't have to immerse ourselves in the strange puzzling paradoxes that always characterize a time of upheaval:

> -the potential for new beginnings born from
>   the loss of treasured pasts,
> -the grief of dreams dying with the
>   exhilaration of what now might be,
> -the impotence and rage of failed ideals and
>   the power of new aspirations,
> -the horrors inflicted on so many innocents that
>   call us to greater compassion.

The challenge is to refuse to categorize ourselves. We don't have to take sides or define ourselves as either optimists or pessimists. Much better to dwell in uncertainty, hold the paradoxes, live in the complexities and contradictions without needing them to resolve.

This is what uncertainty feels like and it's a very healthy place to dwell.

Finding Our Place

Humans have a responsibility to their own time,
not as if they could seem to stand outside it
and donate various spiritual and material benefits
to it from a position of compassionate distance.
Humans have a responsibility to find themselves
where they are, in their own proper time and place,
in the history to which they belong and
to which they must inevitably contribute
either their response or their evasions,
either truth and act,
or mere slogan and gesture.

Thomas Merton
Catholic monk, writer, activist

How did I get so lucky
to have my heart awakened
to others and their suffering?

Pema Chödrön
Buddist teacher

History Chooses you

It is strange but familiar to hear people who are now well-known activists and respected workers for noble causes describe themselves as "accidental activists."

They tell how a compulsion entered them, a clarity that they had to do this work. They say: "I couldn't not do it" or "If I didn't do something, I felt I would go crazy" or "Before I even realized what I was doing, I was doing it."

In every case, they saw an injustice or tragedy or possibility when others weren't aware of a thing. They heard a thundering call that nobody else noticed.

Why this happens is a puzzlement, but it seems that issues choose us. They summon us to pay attention while others stay oblivious. They prompt us to act while others stay asleep. They offer us dreams of bold new futures that others will never see.

We are both blessed and cursed when history chooses us.

But once chosen, we can't *not* do it.

The Right Thing

I was grounded in that moral fiber of
wanting to do the right thing. I was so
sure that this was the right thing because
it was so obvious and even those who
were persecuting me knew, and I knew
they knew...I was doing the right thing.
But they didn't want me to do it
because it was inconveniencing them,
and I knew that.

Wangari Maathai
Noble Peace Laureate 2004

There is a vitality, a life force, a quickening
that is translated through you into action,
and because there is only one of you in all time,
this expression is unique. And if you block it,
it will never exist through any other
medium and it will be lost...

Martha Graham
Dancer/choreographer

Naming Myself

We often choose a name that seems accurate for us, but that isn't big enough to contain our entire life. Often such names describe who or where we've been, but not where we're going. Names such as: "cancer survivor," "victim of war," "displaced person," "child of a dysfunctional family."

What is a name that calls you into your future life?

What is a name that can sustain you for the challenges you will inevitably face? A name that supports you to encounter life's difficulties, not as a victim, but as one who grows stronger and wiser?

What is a name that calls you to be fearless?"

The term "spiritual warrior" is one such name. This is not a traditional warrior, but one of a very different type. Spiritual warriors are "those who are brave." Most importantly, spiritual warriors never use aggression or violence to accomplish their work.

The skills that give them power are compassion and insight. It takes years of practice and discipline to cultivate these. And a strong commitment that these are the skills most needed.

Those who devote the time and exert the discipline to acquire these skills trust themselves to be of service to this troubled time.

It becomes a dark time when
we lose faith in each other and thus lack courage.

Chögyam Trungpa
Buddist teacher

Never Too Late

Bravery is a choice. It is a decision to enter into the fray no matter how illogical and crazy things are. Even as our friends, family and common sense recommend that we stay away.

In our life, we are surrounded by people, events, circumstances that offer continuous proof of how bad things are, including bad people who don't seem worth struggling for.

We did not plan to live in such a crazed world. Very few of us have been prepared by life circumstances to deal with the levels of fear, aggression and insanity we now encounter daily.

When we were being trained to think, to plan, to lead, the world was portrayed as rational, predictable, logical.

But now? Ever present insanity, illogic, injustice, illusion.

This is just the way it is and will continue to be.

We can't restore sanity to the world, but we can still remain sane and available.

We can still aspire to be of service wherever need summons us. We can still focus our energy on working for good people and good causes.

It is never too late to be brave.

Only Don't Know

There is only the fight to recover what has been lost
And found and lost again and again: and now, under
       conditions
That seem unpropitious. But perhaps neither gain nor loss.
For us, there is only the trying. The rest is not our business.

T. S. Eliot
Poet

PART TWO

Let go of the Shore

Know that the river has its destination.
The elders say we must let go of the shore.
Push off into the middle of the river,
and keep our heads above water.

A supernova is a stellar explosion that occurs
at the end of a star's lifetime, when its nuclear fuel
is exhausted and it is no longer supported by the
release of nuclear energy. Supernovae are extremely
luminous and cause a burst of radiation that often
briefly outshines an entire galaxy before fading from
view over several weeks or months.
During this short interval, a supernova can radiate
as much energy as the sun could emit over its life span.

F.W. Giacobbe
Astrophysicist

Eagerness

It's hard to find fault with eagerness. It seems like such a good thing—people motivated and eager to get to work, take on a project, change their lives.

But not too far down the road, eagerness shows its ugly side. People become so committed to their cause or work that they become missionaries. They want everyone to work on this particular issue, or do this diet, or follow this plan that will change your life.

People also can let their commitment to being of service grow into exaggerated heroism. They're willing to take on any problem you give them. They keep looking for the next great cause. They seem unstoppable in their motivation and energy. "Bring it on!" is their life slogan.

Such people are like supernovas—great clouds of fiery, burning gasses that appear powerful and beautiful, but are actually already dead. They've exhausted their energy, blown themselves up and what we're observing in the night sky is just their last gaseous remains.

Eagerness is a good place to start, but its propensity for unfettered growth requires vigilance. Like a parasite, it tends to kill off its host.

It's not a bad thing when our eagerness fades and we find ourselves just doing the work, bored at times, motivated at others, working day-by-day on little tasks, hoping that some of what we're doing is useful, but not really sure.

It's good not to be a supernova.

Just being with your fear,
just being it,
is the most powerful form of fearlessness.

Jerry Granelli
Musician

Fearlessness

Human history is filled with stories of countless people who have been fearless. If we look at our own families, perhaps going back several generations, we'll find among our own ancestors those who also have been fearless. They may have been immigrants who risked to find a better future, veterans who courageously fought in wars, families who endured economic hardships, persecution, slavery, oppression, dislocation.

We all carry within us this lineage of fearlessness.

There's a difference between courage and fearlessness. Courage emerges in the moment, without time for thought. Our heart opens and we immediately move into action. Someone jumps into an icy lake to save a child, or speaks up at a meeting, or puts themself in danger to help another human being. These sudden and heroic actions, even if they put us at risk, arise from clear, spontaneous love.

Fearlessness, too, has love at its core, but it requires a great deal more of us than instant action. If we react too quickly when we feel afraid, we either flee or act aggressively. True fearlessness requires that we take time and exercise discernment. Then we can move with love into right action.

Fearlessness demands that we take time to look at whatever feels threatening to us in all its complexity. We step into the fear, into the moment, and watch how by acknowledging and moving closer, fear dissipates and fearlessness arises.

In the Tibetan tradition, fearlessness is known as an act of ultimate generosity, one of the great gifts we offer others.

Anger gives the illusion of clarity. A certain
strength arises when we have an opinion
and we know where we stand.
The difference between the clarity we believe
we have when angry and the clarity that results from
actually seeing clearly is that aggression has its own
narrow logic, which does not take into account the
deeper level of causes and conditions that
surround each situation.

Dzigar Kongtrul
Buddhist teacher

Righteous Anger

Anger is not a naturally occurring phenomenon. It's important to remember this in this age when we have an abundance of anger available everywhere. So many people are angry about so many things and at so many people. Anger has become not only tolerated, but expected. Perhaps even respected.

Some anger seems well deserved—we call it "righteous anger." Confronted with injustice, genocide, dehumanization, oppression, (the list goes on and on), we have every right to be angry. And this is true— we should be angry and horrified.

Some people are motivated by anger—their sense of outrage seems to energize them and propels them to join ever more causes.

But just how far can anger carry us? And where do we end up? Anger is a primary cause of burn-out and depression. It doesn't give us energy. It eats away at us and makes us sick—there's no nourishment coming into our bodies, such as is so readily available when we feel peaceful, centered, generous.

Anger also clouds our perception. We can see victims, enemies, immoral acts from far off. But what are we missing with our telescopic rage?

Anger separates us from solutions to the problems that make us angry. We can't see the people we need to involve and the information we need to know if we are to resolve any of these terrible situations.

There's no such thing as righteous anger.

Anger in any form only makes us blind.

At one community meeting, we ran into a high-conflict issue.
We ran out of time and agreed to postpone this issue
until the following week. All week, emotions ran high
and opposing views intensified. We eagerly assembled
at the next meeting, impatient to get this issue resolved.
This was a Quaker community—each meeting began
with 5 minutes of silence. On this day, the clerk announced
that, due to the intensity of this issue, we would not begin
with our usual 5 minutes of silence. We all breathed
a sigh of relief, only to hear her announce:
"Today, we'll begin with 20 minutes of silence."

Story told by Parker Palmer
Educator and writer

Urgency Urgency

Urgency is the unavoidable companion of crisis. It seems to be a valuable relationship—crises demand immediate attention and response. Often, the more we know about a situation, the more urgent we become. We have to do something now! Our concern and love needs to be instantly translated into action, otherwise it will seem we don't care.

When we work from this place of urgency, we set ourselves up for failure. We work very hard, push our agenda, get aggressive when we think we need to, and end up more exhausted than effective.

And we get angry. Anyone who doesn't respond immediately becomes our enemy. They may actually be wise people who caution patience, who have a longer-term perspective. But we can't hear their wisdom or experience; we're too anxiously engaged in our cause. We hastily judge them as being in denial or just looking for an excuse not to get involved.

Those who advise proceeding more slowly are not the problem. Our aggression is. Captured by a sense of urgency, we create categories—those for and against us, those who get it, those who don't. Enemies proliferate. As they increase in number, we respond with greater ferocity. We have to fight even harder because there's so much opposition to our just cause.

This is the predictable cycle of urgency. Because things can't wait, we fall into bad behaviors: we proceed full force, shoving people out of the way, ignoring signals, refusing to behave more moderately or modestly. Instead, we martyr ourselves for the cause and fight back with ever greater intensity. In all this ferocious activity, we fail to notice that it's our own behaviors that are intensifying the opposition.

Stop.

Urgency leads nowhere except into the wilderness of aggression and failure. It doesn't serve our cause. It doesn't serve anything.

Not being lost is not a matter of getting back
to where you started from;
it is a decision not to be lost
wherever you happen to find yourself.
It's simply saying, "I'm not lost, I'm right here."

Laurence Gonzales
Author

Lost

When we are overwhelmed and confused, our brains barely function. We reach for the old maps, the routine responses, what worked in the past. This is a predictable response, yet also suicidal.

If we keep grasping for things to look familiar, if we frantically try and fit new problems and situations into old ways of thinking, we will continue to wander lost and eventually collapse from our confusion. There is no way to get out of this wilderness except to acknowledge that we're lost.

Recognizing our situation usually leads at first to even wilder grasping after old solutions. Yet there's nothing we can learn about this strange new world until we stop grasping, pause, calm down, and look around. The first thing we could notice is the most essential: we're still here. This in and of itself makes our situation workable. We don't have to panic about our situation—we need to acknowledge it. Yes, we're lost. But in truth we're not. We're right here.

As we relax enough to tune in, we'll be able to notice the information and signals that are everywhere around us. There's sufficient information right here to help us find our way out. But we have to be willing to stop, to listen, to admit we don't know.

To navigate life today, we definitely need new maps. Our old ones confuse us unendingly. These new maps are waiting for us. They'll appear as soon as we quiet down and, with other lost companions, relax into the unfamiliarity of this new place, senses open, curious rather than afraid.

The maps we need are in us, but not in only one of us. If we read the currents and signs together, we'll find our way through.

Only she who is ready to question,
to think for herself, will find the truth.
To understand the currents of the river,
he who wishes to know the truth
must enter the water.

Nisargadatta
Indian mystic, born 1897

Non-Denial

Looking reality in the eye is an interesting experience. Often, people are startled to realize how much information they've been avoiding, and how much information is out there, waiting to be useful.

"Facts are friendly," a psychologist once said, but most of us don't see it this way. We move away from all the information that's available, we retreat into denial. It's the way we keep our world intact and avoid being challenged or threatened. If we can just hold onto our opinions and views, the world will continue to work just fine, thank you very much.

We get led into the practice of non-denial by failure and defeat. When we have no choice, we seem to get curious. When our back is against the wall, finally we're willing to look at all the messages we had avoided. This isn't a graceful process. But when we're ready to open to the signals, guidance, and information that have been swirling around us, ignored and unnoticed, it's amazing what we learn.

And it's remarkable what capacities we develop. Absorbing these messages, we suddenly see things differently. We discover solutions not available from our former position. We experience surprise, sometimes delight, sometimes despair that we didn't notice things earlier. But the end result is that we become more open, more engaged, and more intelligent.

We learn where we are. From *here*, much more is possible.

Anything more than the truth
would be too much.

Robert Frost
Poet

Self-Deception

Being honest with ourselves is part of the practice of non-denial. Trying to see ourselves without deception becomes especially important if we're engaged in serving the world. The world has such great needs, and we truly want to help. It's hard not to develop a myth about ourselves and our capacity to keep going—a false self-assessment bound to get us in trouble.

Our personal myths blind us to knowing what we can and can't do. What are our limits? How much more work, how many more causes can we realistically take on? How exhausted are we? What signals from our bodies are we denying? How much longer can we keep this up? Do we think we're doing just fine playing the lone hero?

And finally, why are we afraid to ask these questions? Do we feel that once we see the truth we'll just run away or withdraw or abandon everything and everybody?

Of course, seeing clearly who we are in this moment—our health, our motivation, the messages coming from our world—gives us the information we need to continue on.

Just not in a self-destructive savior mode.

It was like this:
you were happy, then you were sad,
then happy again, then not.

Jane Hirshfield
Poet

Back and Forth

We move between extremes feeling

> great then terrible

> energized then exhausted

> successful then a failure

> accepting then resentful

> peaceful then angry

> joyful then despairing.

These shifts don't mean much. Every emotion comes and goes, often followed by its opposite. Just wait a bit, and you'll see your emotions change. They'll change if you let them, if you don't get all tangled up telling yourself a story about why you feel this way.

We don't have to take our emotions so seriously.

We don't have to act on them.

We don't have to give them so much power over us.

We don't have to hold onto them or be fascinated by them or give them any more than brief attention.

Emotions come and go—this is our human experience. If we wait a moment, if we pause and don't act right away, this too will pass.

It is time for all the heroes to go home
if they have any, time for all of us common ones
to locate ourselves by the real things
we live by.

William Stafford
Poet

Middle

We live in a world of extremes and polarities. People take positions at the far edge of an issue, and then scream across the distance they created. Others, numbed by every-day experience, seek out extremes in sports and personal challenges.

Living at the extreme consumes enormous resources. We spend energy on justifying our position, on attacking our enemy, on defending our ground, on protecting our position. Or in the case of extreme sports, we devote huge amounts of time and resources to training and preparing for the ultimate challenge.

Somewhere in all the furor and drama, we've lost sight of the middle. Yet it's in the middle where the possibilities reside. Some call the middle "compromise" or "consensus"—terms which have come to mean failure, mediocrity and loss. We don't remember meeting in the middle as anything but negative.

Perhaps because we're so addicted to strong emotions and loud noises to motivate us, we no longer seek the quiet space of center. But all great spiritual traditions speak of moderation, harmony, balance—the middle way.

One way to rediscover middle is to notice your everyday behaviors. Notice where you're positioned on an issue important to you. Are you sitting out on one side, justifying your behavior, assuming you're right and others are wrong? Or are you open to the possibility that you can't see very well from where you're sitting, that you don't know all the facts in the case?

Humility and curiosity is what shifts us to center. Just by being curious, we move toward the middle ground, with its fertile promise of new ideas and new relationships.

Everything Changes

Yin-yang is the ancient Taoist symbol of life, the dance of opposition that creates wholeness, the dance that never ends. This timeless symbol depicts not only the dance, but the relationship between opposites, how opposition works.

One state gives birth to the other. Whichever state is here this moment, we can be sure that what's coming next will be its opposite.

The symbol also describes a subtle but essential dynamic of life. When a condition reaches its fullness, when its dominance is at maximum power, it's then that its opposite state begins to emerge.

At first, the new birth is just a sliver, a new moon glimmer of the future. But the dominant will now begin to wane, and the new will grow. Eventually, it too will become the overbearing present and it too will give birth to the next newness.

In this way, life's ceaseless dynamic of change offers hope and caution simultaneously. Everything changes. Good times don't last forever. And neither do bad ones. Whatever is happening now, good or bad, is giving birth to the next state, which will be its opposite.

Does knowledge of this dance help us persevere?

If you maintain a sense of humor and a distrust of the rules
laid down around you, there will be success.

Chögyam Trungpa
Buddhist teacher

No Big Deal

Most people have had the experience of being focused on something that seemed incredibly important, such as deciding what to buy or choosing what color to paint a wall, then suddenly having that dilemma swept away by learning that someone they love is seriously ill.

This instantaneous shift in priorities applies to nearly every situation in life, even the current crisis that's overwhelming you right now, that feels so critically important to resolve *now*.

Today's crisis is guaranteed to shift and change. We can count on this. Without any help from us, situations lose their "big deal" status, shoved aside by the next crisis. In part, this is evidence that we live in a constantly changing universe. But it's also true because we live in a leadership culture that seems addicted to crisis. Too many leaders want to know about every little crisis, yet never focus long enough on any one to resolve it. So why should we be the ones making it into a big deal right now if tomorrow it will be demoted or forgotten?

"No big deal" is an attitude that serves us well in life and in work. But it's important to note what it doesn't mean. It doesn't mean being numb to what's happening or what demands our attention. It doesn't mean shrugging our shoulders and walking away. It doesn't mean saying, "Oh well, that's just the way it is."

We absolutely need to pay attention to crises and issues, and we need to be fully engaged with them for the long-term. But we don't need to over-inflate the issue in a way that obscures clear seeing and right action. We don't need to fill the crisis with urgency, which only promotes confusion and aggression.

In the greater scheme of things, this current crisis truly is no big deal. With that recognition, we can do very good work.

If you can't get destination,
go for direction.

James Gimian
Publisher

Destination

Most of us think we know where we're going. Or at least we think we *should* know where we're going. We may have been taught about goal or intention-setting, perhaps even about planning and strategic thinking.

Knowing where we want to end up seems essential. As one wit said: "If you don't know where you're going, you may just end up there."

But once we know what our destination is—in life or love or this project—we too easily get trapped by desire. Holding our hopes tightly, intent on reaching our goal, working to implement the plan, to reach our dream—all this focus and dedication places huge blinders on us. We may be diligent, but we're also dangerously myopic.

And it severely inhibits our relationship with life. We're so intent on getting somewhere, or performing well, or becoming someone in particular, that we shut out and shut down. We silence the messages coming from our world. We don't take in information, we just plow ahead with evermore determination.

Good-bye to curiosity, farewell to experimentation. Welcome in disappointment, failure, regret.

We could lighten up—we could go for direction, not destination. We could invite in what the world seems to want for us, what it's offering us right here, right now

We could enjoy what we'll see and discover when we take off the blinders of non-negotiable destination.

The basic difference between an ordinary person
and a warrior is that a warrior takes everything
as a challenge, while an ordinary person
takes everything as a blessing or as a curse.

Don Juan, Carlos Casteneda

Steadfastness

Steadfastness is a lovely, old-fashioned word that we don't hear much about these days. It describes how warriors stand their ground, how they find their position and stay there, unshaken and immovable. Steadfast people are firm in their resolve; they are not shaken by events or circumstances. They stand clear in their beliefs, grounded in their cause, faithful to the end.

Steadfast people seem very rare these days, a distinct minority in the flood of opportunistic, self-serving, priority-switching, disloyal people we encounter daily. And we may question our own steadfastness. But there are enough of us out there, people who place a value on steadfastness and want to learn how to develop it.

It's fine for steadfast people to be the minority. The world always and only changes from the actions and commitment of "a small group of dedicated people," as sociologist Margaret Mead stated so clearly years ago. Instead of being distracted by all the unsteadfast ones, we need to actively search for each other and expect we'll find us.

Yet we will have to look in new places—among those we've discounted and misjudged, those who disappeared from our awareness months or years ago. We have to look again, and be willing to be surprised by who we see.

And once we find each other, we need to support and encourage our steadfast behaviors—the times when any one of us speaks up, stands our ground, sees clearly, refuses to yield, doesn't give up.

Steadfastness is a capacity that gets easier as we're together. The ground we stand on gets more firm and offers more support. It expands to uphold a surprising number of spiritual warriors.

The solution is never about fixing
but about staying...
with the fear of helplessness
and loss of control.

Ezra Bayda
Zen teacher

Staying

After we've tried and tried and only failed, we usually want to get out of there as fast as we can, find a new project, a new partner, a new place. Anything to forget our failure and frustration.

Of course, even as we scramble for a new chance to feel successful, we know there's no escape, that we take ourselves with us wherever we go.

Yet how do we resist the compulsion to grasp after new things, to find security elsewhere—anything to get out of the mess we're in?

All we have to do is acknowledge that we're helpless, that things are not under our control. Simple.

Some describe this as surrender, or yielding, or giving in. These aren't capacities we've thought of as strengths. But they keep us in the turbulence, they enable us to stay.

Ironically, we find the strength to stay by realizing that there's nothing we can accomplish by staying.

And there we are, still in the middle of the river, hoping to be ready for what's next.

Every day I have to make
a choice not to give up.

Non-profit CEO

Choosing

Perseverance is a choice. It's not a simple, one-time choice, it's a daily one. There's never a final decision.

Our first "yes"—filled with energy and enthusiasm—brought us here, but it's of no use as the waters rise and the turbulence increases. By the time we're surrounded by obstacles and opposition, by aggression and mean-spiritedness, our initial choice has no meaning (if we can even remember that optimistic moment).

This is as it should be. Having to make a choice every day keeps us alert and present. Do I have the resources, internal and external, to keep going? Can I deal with what's in front of me right now? Do I have any patience left? Is there a way through this mess?

These critical questions require a momentary pause, a little reflection. Rather than just striking out or being reactive to a bad day, we offer ourselves freedom. Do I continue or do I give up? Even a brief pause creates the space for freedom. We're not trapped by circumstances or fatigue. We give ourselves a moment to look as clearly as we can at the current situation.

And then we make a conscious choice. Every day.

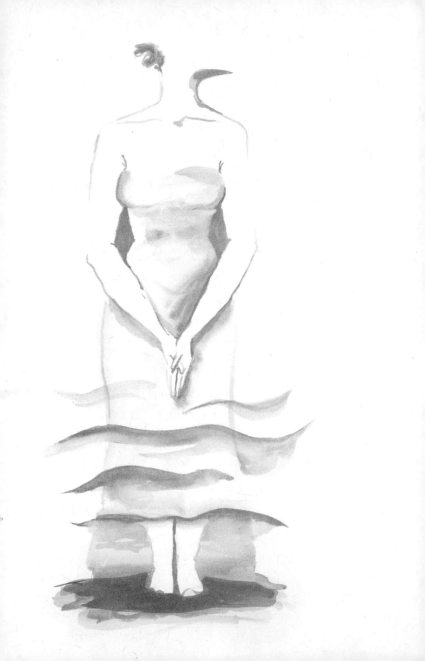

PART THREE

Take nothing Personally

And I say see who is there with you and celebrate.
At this time in history, we are to take nothing personally,
least of all ourselves,
for the moment we do,
our spiritual growth and journey come to a halt

Only as a warrior can one withstand the path of knowledge.
A warrior cannot complain or regret anything.
His life is an endless challenge, and challenges
cannot possibly be good or bad.
Challenges are simply challenges.

Don Juan, Carlos Castenada

Emotions

Many of us have spent years learning to notice our emotional responses. And we've raised our children to be aware of when they feel sad or angry or frustrated. Western culture focuses our attention endlessly on noticing and working with our internal state.

This is helpful, up to a point. It's important not to deny any of our feelings, both the good and bad ones. But there's a crucial next step: we have to realize that we authored these emotional responses. We made them up, so we can change them.

Emotions don't exist independent of us—it's not as if anger or grief float around looking for victims to inhabit. Everything we feel and experience comes from inside us. How we respond to any situation or person depends on what's happened to us in the past and, most importantly, what interpretations we've given to those experiences.

We walk around wrapped in our stories, and it only takes a small poke from the outside world to unleash a flood of them in all their velocity. Over time, we become packages of predictable responses. We forget there's any other way to respond.

The good news is that at any moment we can refuse to be triggered in the old, familiar ways. This takes practice, and a lot of discipline, but the next time you find yourself gripped by any strong emotion, see if you can just observe the feeling. Don't deny it or judge it. Don't start telling yourself *why* you're angry or sad. Just observe that you are. If you can avoid, even for a moment, getting dragged under by your usual storyline, that's real progress. You've succeeded in bringing in just a tiny bit of air, a momentary breath—and in that small opening lies the possibility of freedom.

We illuminate the road to freedom each time we make a conscious choice to stay out of our stories. The road gets easier to see in the light of each pause.

This has been going on through the ages.

They criticize the silent ones.

They criticize the talkative ones.

They criticize the moderate ones.

There is no one in the world who escapes criticism.

There never was and never will be,

nor is there now,

the wholly criticized

or the wholly approved.

Buddha

Praise and Blame

There is absolutely no way to avoid being criticized. Nobody gets through life described as totally wonderful.

The question is, what do we do with criticism? Do we take it in, believe it and develop self-loathing? Do we assume that a criticism of something we've done is a condemnation of who we are?

Or can we filter criticism and keep it focused as perhaps valuable but bounded information? Can we look for the kernels of truth there that might help us improve? Can we not instantly push criticism away, yet not accept it totally?

And can we treat praise the same way, not instantly basking in our glory? Praise and blame are two sides of the same coin. If we are eager to accept praise, then we are equally vulnerable to feel the sting of blame.

In both cases, we need to listen with caution and discernment. There are truths in what people say about us, good and bad, but let's not ever believe that their words define us.

Fall down 53 times.
Get up 54.

Zen slogan

Failure

Failure is unavoidable. There's no way to avoid times of crushing defeat, great loss, terrible regret. We might like to think that "failure is not an option," but it's guaranteed to appear and reappear throughout our lives. This is just how life works.

It helps to know this ahead of time. Or to learn it very quickly. What's essential is how we work with failure, what we do once its ugly face appears.

Some people feel that failure is a lesson sent by God to teach them what they need to learn. Others feel that failure is a punishment meted out to them by God or destiny. To some it's karma. Whatever your personal view, failure certainly is an opportunity to learn—not just about yourself, but about how the world works. Failure is filled with messages. How we interpret those messages is critical to what happens next.

When we fail, we have the opportunity to feel really bad about ourselves. Often, our own negativity is encouraged by others telling us how worthless we are, how everything that's gone wrong is our fault.

But we could learn more helpful and realistic things. We could learn that every failure results from a complexity of factors. It's never just one person's fault. We could learn about ourselves, what triggers us, which of our behaviors create problems, which seem helpful. We could learn about the dynamics and patterns present in the situation that had an impact on its negative outcome.

It takes a lot of contributions from many different sources to create failure. We're wasting the opportunity to learn and grow if we try to pin the blame on just one person or one reason.

The practice countermeasure to blame
is to directly face the pain
we are trying to avoid.

Ezra Bayda
Zen teacher

Blame

When things go wrong, we're conditioned in Western culture to turn on each other. If we can just find someone to blame, or determine a simple explanation to our difficulty, we can move on.

If only life were that simple.

The world doesn't work this logically or straightforwardly. It's never just one person's fault, no matter how terrible or nasty they are.

The search for scapegoats is a huge detour from the work that has to be done, the problem that has to be solved. And it deprives us of the energy and relationships we need.

Seeking scapegoats or hastily assigning blame tears us apart. How can we trust one another if we think that someone's about to accuse us of something we didn't do?

Rather than hunt for a hapless victim, what if we all could admit that we're deeply troubled by what's happened, that we're all feeling distressed by this turn of events.

If we directly face the pain of what's here in our midst, we won't become blinded by blame. Past the pain is the possibility of clear-seeing, unclouded by despair or paranoia.

From here, we can see the way forward. Together

Fear is the cheapest room in the house.
I would like to see you living
in better conditions.

Hafiz
Sufi teacher, poet, 14th century

Fear

Fear is just part of human life. It's so common that every great spiritual tradition includes the injunction: "Be not afraid."

If fear is this fundamental to being human, we can expect that we'll feel afraid at times, perhaps even frequently. Yet when fear appears, we don't have to worry that we've failed, or take it as a sign that we're not as good as other people. In fact, we're just like other people. Fear is simple evidence that we're human.

What's important to decide is what we do with our fear. We can withdraw, flee, distract or numb ourselves. Or we can acknowledge that we're scared. And stay right here.

We can stay where we are and bravely investigate our fear. We can move toward it, curious about it. We can even interview it. What does it feel like? What color is it? Does it have a texture, size, personality?

What's important is to question the fear itself. We're not asking ourselves *why* we feel afraid, which is our usual inquiry. We just want to know more about this seemingly frightful creature that showed up in us.

Our investigation moves us closer and closer, and then the fear begins to change. Paradoxically, the more we engage directly with it, the less fearful it becomes.

It is our curiosity that transforms fear. Most often, it dissolves into energy that we can work with.

And all because we were willing to develop a relationship with what, at first, appeared so frightening.

If we could read the secret history
of those we would like to punish,
we would find in each life a sorrow and suffering
enough to disarm all our hostility.

Henry Wadsworth Longfellow
Writer, poet

Aggression

One way to look at aggression is as gestures. Thinking of the motions of aggression, rather than the causes, can be helpful. At any moment, if we notice these movements, we can prevent ourselves from going where aggression wants to take us.

Aggression begins as a gesture of separation; we draw a line and create an antagonist, a threat, an enemy. Aggression must have an object to fight, to strike out against or to defend ourselves from.

Thus one way to interrupt aggression is to move closer to the object we fear. We might ask a question or become curious about our enemy's motivation. Getting a bit closer through our curiosity, we might discover that we and the stranger have shared a similar life experience—a realization of our common humanity.

Whenever we go on the attack, verbally or physically, aggression becomes another gesture, that of a projectile, something like a heat-seeking missile intent on finding its target.

Once we launch, we can curtail our aggression by stopping the forward motion. In a confrontation, in a hallway or meeting room, we can back-up just a few inches. Or it can be as simple as sitting back in the chair rather than leaning aggressively across the table or desk.

Or we can notice the spear–like precision of our language as we go in for the attack. Instead of words intent on cutting and destroying, we could choose plump phrases, gentler words that have no sharp edges.

One gesture to counteract aggression comes from the 8th century Buddhist teacher Shantideva. He advised us to 'sit like a log' when we get provoked and want to react. Even if we sit there feeling more like a crocodile trying to camouflage itself as a log, it helps to pause, get quiet, and just wait for our reactions to subside.

Love is the only emotion that
expands intelligence.

Humberto Maturana
Scientist

Jealousy

Jealousy and generosity are reverse images of one another. In response to any circumstance, one or the other will arise, guaranteed. Since they inhabit the same space, only one can appear at any time; they cancel each other out. Jealousy arises as generosity disappears, generosity flourishes as jealousy is stilled.

When something good happens to someone else—another organization wins a grant, a friend gets a promotion, someone else gets the opportunity we wanted—we can activate either emotion. We can question whether there's enough to go around. We can wonder whose need is greater, or just assume that we needed it more. We can be happy for their good fortune, or bemoan the loss of ours.

As closely connected as jealousy and generosity are, they create very different consequences. If jealousy predominates, we turn inward, shrivel our hearts, and lose strength. If generosity grows, we grow also. Our world expands. We realize there's enough to go round. We realize we don't need everything we thought we did. The world in general feels more reliable, more trustworthy, more enjoyable.

The world expands from the inside out—it's our hearts that have enlarged. We not only feel more loving, we're also more open and aware. We see more, we take in more, we let in more.

Jealousy is such a waste of a good human heart.

The trouble with the rat race is that even if you win,
you're still a rat.

Lily Tomlin, Comedienne/Author

Boredom

Current culture places no value on boredom. In fact, it gives it absolutely no respect. Moments of nothingness, of not-doing, not-knowing—these are to be avoided at all costs. Lucky for us, we have the pocket technology to guarantee that we never lapse into boredom, not even for one second.

Yet boredom is a doorway, an invitation to step into uncluttered, nothing-there space. From the outside, it doesn't look at all appealing. We instantaneously reject the invitation and look for something more evidently stimulating.

But boredom offers a lot. For one thing, it can give our frantic exhausted selves some rest. We don't have to do anything. We can just sit there and rest in the open space of nothing-to-do. If we can rest there, we might learn to stop fearing this unfamiliar emptiness. We might start to enjoy some of its qualities, such as coolness, peacefulness, tranquility.

Into this new empty space, many temptations will appear, things we need to do, ideas we need to write down immediately, people we need to contact, and lists, lists, lists.

But we don't have to respond to any of these. We can continue to just sit there, becoming a little more familiar with this cool, quiet sensation of doing nothing.

Later, we can get busy again.

People are too busy to care.

Healthcare worker

Laziness

Laziness is a choice, like most things in life. It's choosing the easier way out, the path of least consciousness. But while laziness is easy to notice when we don't want to do physical work, it's actually everywhere in our lives—in the pivotal choices we make about our emotions, our reactions and where we focus our attention.

For example, being angry or depressed is a common form of laziness. When we begin to feel these emotions at the fringes of our awareness, it's easier to surrender to them than work to prevent them from getting a firm foothold inside us. Even though we may fear the consequences of anger or depression, we're very familiar with them. It requires no work whatsoever to let them take over. That's laziness.

We also slip into laziness about our habits and routines. Even if we're unhappy with the life we've created by succumbing to these routines, it takes work to change them. It's easier to just let them continue on and keep beating ourselves up. That's laziness.

Busyness is another form of laziness. As long as we're working hard, we don't have to exert any effort to notice whether our work is working, whether it's leading anywhere good. We don't have to pay attention to what's happening, who's affected, who's reacting, what the unintended consequences are that clutter the path behind us. We just keep going, busy, thoughtless, ineffective.

Laziness lulls us into a life we don't like, even though we let it happen because we thought it would be easier. Unconsciously, we chose boredom and routine over life itself.

Life takes work. Awareness takes work. So does perseverance.

So let us plant dates, even though
we who plant them will never eat them.
We must live by the love of what we will never see.
This is the secret of discipline.

Rubem Alvez
Brazilian theologian

Discipline

Discipline is a strange and foreign concept to many people today. We've been conditioned to follow our passion, to do what we love, to connect our work with our life's purpose so that we'll be highly motivated.

But life doesn't work this way, and work doesn't get done this way. After the first rush of romance in discovering meaningful work, there's the actual work to be done. The work will, at times, be boring, repetitive, uninteresting, senseless.

This is why discipline is so important. If you have a daily regimen—exercise, meditation, prayer, sports, music, writing—you've learned to do the same thing day after day. You don't abandon it when it gets boring. You don't avoid the repetition. You learn to just do it, because you know that the repetition and boredom eventually serve your goal.

When engaged in this kind of practice, at some point we realize that tomorrow will be just like today, and there's nothing more to do than finish today so we can begin again tomorrow. We practice, practice, practice, focused on completing the session we're in right now.

If our life lacks this kind of discipline, we end up always looking for a substitute. We seek new work, new causes, new relationships, something or somebody that will fire up our passion and make us feel motivated and alive again.

Propelled by passion rather than by discipline, we end up spent, exhausted, unhappy.

And we lose the capacity to persevere.

Nothing can temper the spirit of a warrior
as much as the challenge of dealing
with impossible people in positions of power.
Only under those conditions can warriors
acquire the sobriety and serenity to
withstand the pressure of the unknowable.

Don Juan, Carlos Castaneda

Stupidity

How do we deal with what appears sometimes as stupidity, and other times as deliberately feigned ignorance? How do we deal with people who refuse to understand, who seem to just want to make our lives more difficult, who keep asking the same questions over and over but who never understand our answers no matter how many times we explain things?

Even if we've learned to stop being so reactive and can keep our strong emotions under control, stupidity demands a whole other level of patience and practice. Especially if we feel that the person is playing dumb deliberately in order to block our work.

There certainly are people who consciously choose to misunderstand our work. But we often encounter something else—a genuine inability to understand us that is not caused by mental incapacity or nasty intention, but by humans' inherent perceptual inability to see anything that is truly new and different. Any work, proposal or idea that comes from a different worldview, that is based on a new way of thinking, creates lots of "stupid" people.

It's not that they can't reason, think or apply logic. It's that they have no framework for understanding anything based on different beliefs and assumptions, different logic. When people look at new ideas through their familiar lens, all they see is a haze of disconnected statements and ideas. And it's not about helping them connect the dots—we're presenting ideas that, to them, don't even look like dots.

Patience is the only remedy for this situation. And compassion. Let's not judge them as stupid or difficult or obstinate. Let's redefine our task and challenge ourselves to become gentle guides to the world as we see it, not fierce advocates for our view of reality.

Then we'll discover there's less stupidity blocking our path.

[The basic order of life] includes all the aspects of life—
including those that are ugly and bitter and sad.
But even those qualities are part of the rich fabric of
existence that can be woven into our being. In fact, we
are already woven into that fabric whether we like it
or not...We cannot change the way the world is,
but by opening ourselves to the world as it is,
we may find that gentleness, decency, and bravery
are available—not only to us, but to all human beings.

Chögyam Trungpa
Buddhist teacher

Loneliness

If we're set on creating change, on doing things differently, we must be prepared for loneliness. As someone noted, "It's lonely to get to the future first." We can't expect to be joined by a lot of people. We will always be the minority, and we will always feel invisible and lonely.

Or at least we'll feel this way at first. As our work deepens and we find the few others to accompany us, as we grow wiser about how the world works and lower our expectations of what might be possible to accomplish, our emotional state becomes less compelling. We pay less attention to how we're feeling. We just keep doing the work.

We don't develop this wisdom and patience without experiencing many difficult times when we feel abandoned, ignored, maligned, and unloved. But we can pass through these, or more accurately, we can let these feelings pass through us, without responding, without telling ourselves a story. If we can avoid justifying our emotions, if we can avoid explaining *why* we feel so badly, our emotions won't solidify into a story that keeps us down. These feelings will pass, if we let them.

Loneliness eventually transforms into a willingness to be alone, even a desire for the space and peace available when nobody else is there. But to get to this lovely place, we first have to let loneliness be there, wait for it to pass through, and then notice that it's gone, that we quite like the space we're in.

Everything changes, even the harshest times and the most terrifying feelings. We can trust this process—it's the only one there is.

Who then devised the torment? Love.
Love is the unfamiliar Name
Behind the hands that wove
The intolerable shirt of flame
Which human power cannot remove.
We only live, only suspire
Consumed by either fire or fire.

T. S. Eliot
Poet

guilt

Mistakes, errors of judgment, hurt and harm we cause others—the path of life is cluttered with these sadnesses we hoped to never cause and certainly never want to happen again.

How do we react when we're disappointed in ourselves?

Disappointment can grow almost without notice into shame, guilt, self-hatred. What began as a mistake, a lapse of judgment or a tragedy caused by inattention consumes us and destroys our future capacity. One moment or period of bad behavior can predict the rest of our life. This is the true tragedy—we never recover, never learn how to keep going.

There's a fundamental distinction between guilt and regret. Guilt turns us inward, creating a cauldron of self-hatred that destroys us. People never act wisely from guilt—the intensity of emotions prevents discernment and right action.

Regret, on the other hand, does not disable us. It gives us the capacity to see clearly, to clarify our future, to change. We can vow to not repeat our mistakes, we can pay attention to what we've learned, we can focus our heart and mind on not causing harm again. We can develop greater insight into who we are, and move forward to become who we'd like to be.

If guilt and shame are driving us inward, hopefully we can notice this direction and choose, even for a moment, to look outward. If we look out into the world, we will notice that millions of other people are, at this very moment, experiencing the same terrible feelings.

We can use this time of feeling badly about ourself to get beyond our self, and connect with all those other humans with whom we share this dark kinship. If our hearts open to them, what enters us is not more darkness, but the light of compassion.

grief

If we are able to give ourselves to the loss,
to move toward it—rather than recoil in an
effort to escape, deny, distract, or obscure—
our wounded hearts become full,
and out of that fullness we will do things differently,
and we will do different things.
Our loss, our wound, is precious to us because it can
wake us up to love, and to loving action.

Norman Fischer
Zen teacher

Do not squander your life.

Zen Evening Reminder

Death

For something that's so obvious—that we all die—it's remarkable how little use we make of our impending demise. Instead of taking advantage of our condition, we try and control it—believing that some-one somewhere will save us from this inevitability.

Accepting death, far ahead of its appearance, is richly liberating. Suddenly we find courage, energy, determination and levels of freedom never available when we were crouched down in self-protection. Accepting death opens us, frees us, clarifies life, simplifies decisions.

But too many of us have yet to discover this. We clutch to life, work to avoid aging, pray not to get sick, and may even avoid those who are ill and dying.

Those who've been visibly brave in the world, those who are known for their tireless efforts for freedom, for the poor, for the planet—all liberated themselves from fearing death. Death might be on their future path, but in this present moment, death has ceased to control them. As one said: "We're all going to die anyway, so we might as well do something with our life."

Can we enjoy the opportunities that death offers? Can we focus on its gifts of clear-seeing, fearlessness and the absolute relishing of this present moment and the people we're with?

Hopefully we can accept these gifts while we still have life enough in us to enjoy them.

PART FOUR

Banish the Word Struggle

The time of the lone wolf is over.
Gather yourselves.
Banish the word struggle from your attitude
and vocabulary.

From a certain point onward,
there is no turning back.
That is the point that must be reached.

Franz Kafka
Writer

Why Stay

It's normal to reach the point where we start questioning our motivation: "Why do I work so hard?" "Why am I dedicating so much time to this?" "Why do I stay in this work?"

And if we don't ask these questions, our friends and loved ones surely will. Usually, if they're confronting us with these, they already have the answers in mind: Stop working so hard; get a life; notice that other people aren't nearly as dedicated as you.

Asking "Why stay?" can be an invitation to reassess not our work load, but our original commitment that brought us into this work. Especially when we're overloaded, burned-out and exhausted, it's extremely helpful to pause occasionally and reflect on the sense of purpose and potential contribution that lured us into working for this cause. Doing this with colleagues who also are working much too hard is a well-tested means for deepening our relationships and strengthening our resolve to keep going.

But there's also a significant element of irrationality in why we keep going, even in the midst of defeat and exhaustion. The question "why?" doesn't lead us to any personal clarity or reassessment, because there really isn't an answer.

We're doing the work because we're doing the work.

If we try and develop an explanation beyond this simple statement of fact, we get into murky waters. Yet even though it's the truth, it's a statement destined to promote either anger or confusion in our loved ones.

It's an insufficient answer, and sometimes it's the only one available.

After the final no there comes a yes
and on that yes the future world depends.

Wallace Stevens
Poet

Giving Up

Sometimes we just need to stop what we're doing and acknowledge that things are not going to work out as we'd like.

Sometimes we need to realize that we've given all we can and we're all used up.

Sometimes we need to acknowledge that we're exhausted and have absolutely no energy left.

How we approach these moments is fundamental to whether we can continue on. Do we feel guilty, upset at ourselves, depressed? Or can we see this moment as rich with information about what's possible and what's not?

Giving up is a moment either of acceptance or resignation, two very different states.

Resignation has a beaten up, victim quality to it. We worked hard and we lost. We've been defeated. Now it's time to retreat, to move on, to put this experience behind us as quickly as possible.

Acceptance is radically different—we're in touch with reality, we've learned that we're not the savior of the situation, and we might feel humbled, but not beaten. We have a richer picture of what's going on and, after a little rest, we'll reenter the fray.

Acceptance is to be relished. It allows us to sink our feet more deeply in the mud, and from there to find real sustenance.

This abiding place, this state of being, of not knowing,
is a very difficult place to be. It's the
place where we don't know what's right, what's
wrong, what's real, what's not real. It's the place of
just being, of life itself, [the place of] no
separation between subject and object, no space
between I and thou, you and me, up and down,
right and wrong.
I call such practice bearing witness.

Bernie Glassman
Zen teacher

Don't Ask Why

When we get into a difficult situation, when we're trying to solve a problem or understand another person's behavior, we shift into analysis. Depending on what we've read or how we've been trained or who our spiritual teacher is, we immediately try and figure out what's going on.

Some of us are exceptionally skilled at this, and also quite happy to offer our assessment to anyone who'll listen (and often to those who won't). Ironically, the more we've trained to be understanding and sensitive, the quicker we are to analyze what's going on. Yet all our tools and techniques are simply judgments.

The very act of analysis is a separation—standing back or outside of the situation in order to grasp it. As we stand outside peering into the problem or the person, we don't even notice how little information we're taking in.

We go looking for certain information and are oblivious to anything else, even when it's staring us in the face. Here is where the practice of not-knowing comes in handy. Can we just dwell with the problem, the person, the emotion?

Can we let in new information, even that which we've pushed away? Can we just be with what is rather than asking why it is? Of course this is very hard, but it's the essence of being in relationship with whatever's going on. Just there, just as present as we can possibly be, available to whatever information wants to be noticed.

Bearing witness.

The world speaks everything to us.
It is our only friend.

William Stafford
Poet

As It Is

Sometimes the best thing to do is just leave things alone. To stop manipulating, interfering or pushing things along with your own worn-out energy. This is the first step—withdrawing your energy from forcing or cajoling.

The next move is to change where you are, to stop looking at the situation from the outside and to step into it as much as you can. From inside, a whole different territory is revealed.

What do you notice when you stand inside the problem and take a look around? What information is available to you when you stop and listen to all the messages being offered? What happens as you stand there as open and curious as you can manage at this time, willing to not-know, even for a second?

Being in not-knowing, open and aware, is how we discover right action—the appropriate means for what needs to happen. Right action usually doesn't match our plans, conceived as they were from outside. But now that we're inside the situation, curious and uncertain, we're able to notice what's here. We begin to see dynamics, people, patterns and information we can work with. We become realistic about what's available. Now we can focus on working with what's here, rather than what we thought we needed.

If we take this approach, in every situation, we discover that the resources we need are already here. We have more than enough to work with. It's our task to notice this abundance, and then figure out how to work with it appropriately. What's possible now, given all these new resources we've discovered?

The situation, no matter how difficult, doesn't need to be different. We just need to see it differently.

A Buddhist teacher caught himself complaining about the loud party nearby that was disturbing his meditation. And then he had this insight "Oh, the sound is just the sound. It is me who is going out to annoy it. If I leave the sound alone, it won't annoy me. It's just doing what it has to do. That's what sound does. It makes sound. That is it's job. So if I don't go out to bother the sound, it's not going to bother me. Aha!"

Story told about Ajahn Chah
Buddhist teacher

Choice

Choice makes the world go round. The only problem is we don't know this. Everything in our world—what we feel, who we like, what we dislike, what we do—is a choice. When we realize this, and start to act on it, we regain our freedom and control. We become more conscious participants in any situation.

We need first to notice that we've made choices about everything in our lives. How we react and respond, every single feeling, is a choice. Every situation has infinite possibilities for interpretation and reaction. But we collapse all those possibilities the second we assign a feeling or judgment to the situation.

How do we get out of this constriction and discover infinite choice?

It begins with recognizing that we're not locked in by our perceptions, that other responses are possible. Instead of deciding we don't like a person, even if the reason seems valid and obvious, we could pause and take another look. Or we could ask them a question that invites them to reveal something more about themselves.

Or on a day when we're beating up on ourselves, or feeling depressed, we could notice that we're telling ourselves a story. At that moment, we could deliberately choose another story, one that's positive, bragging, grateful. It won't be a true story, but none of them are. They're all fictions of our drama queen minds.

Changing the story seems unauthentic, lacking integrity. But in this case, authenticity is very over-rated. And extremely limiting.

Why, in this world of infinite freedom and choice, would we lock ourselves into one petty story, no matter how much time, attention and creativity we've spent on composing it?

Sit down and be quiet. You are drunk.
And this is the edge of the roof.

Rumi
Sufi mystic, poet, 13th century

Stuck

It's unfortunate that life isn't about constant progress and unending success. Life is circular in form—cycles of light and darkness, success and failure, order and chaos. Seldom do we appreciate the necessity for these opposites. We'd rather just have it be successful and wonderful all the time. But we all have to pass through life's cycles, gracefully or not.

When we personally are confronted by the downside of these cycles, such as when we get stuck, how do we respond? Do we get frustrated? Do we become angry and aggressive? Do we immediately find something else to distract and motivate us? Do we search for a scapegoat or target? Do we withdraw and disappear?

Or do we sit there, content to acknowledge that we're stuck, that we have no idea what to do now?

In the workings of life, everything moves between periods of chaos and order. Too long in either state is destructive. Too much chaos and nothing new gets created; too much order and nothing gets accomplished. Stuckness is a sign that there's too much order—too much rigidity in our thinking. It's time to loosen our grip.

When we get stuck, when nothing seems to be moving and there's nothing we can do, this means that a very fruitful time is at hand. But these fruits come at a cost—we have to be willing to let go of what we've been holding onto—our opinions and beliefs, our current ways of perceiving things, our old methods and techniques.

We're inside a large knot and the tighter we hold onto any of its strands, the more stuck we get. Loosening our grip, letting some fresh air into our opinions, bringing in new voices and more diversity—any of these approaches will ease the knotty tension we've created.

It's another opportunity to recognize where we are and relax into the experience. Things will become so much easier if we do.

Want to make God laugh?
Show God your plans.

Bumper sticker

Control

What do we control in life, truthfully?

Even a quick glance at our day-to-day life reveals our constant attempts at control—interactions with our children or partner, planning a meeting, developing a project, rehearsing how to approach someone about a situation. And we seek control for a very good reason. We know better. We know what needs to be done.

Just about every person alive is a dismal failure at control. No matter how clever or dedicated we are, everybody resists our best efforts to control them, and life does too. Our failure isn't due to poor technique or lack of information or lack of respect.

Life simply is uncontrollable.

There is only one thing we can control in life—our own self. We can control our thoughts, our emotions, our responses. We can observe our behaviors and reactions and realize we made a choice. Therefore, we could choose a different response. If we have ourselves under control.

This is not about repressing or denying our experience. Quite the opposite. It's about looking in the right place for where control is valid, where control can make a difference.

Because, if we learn to control ourselves, the entire world around us changes.

GLOBAL WARMING

When his ship first came to Australia,
Cook wrote; the natives
Continued fishing, without looking up.
Unable, it seems, to fear what was too large to be comprehended.

Jane Hirshfield
Poet

Invisibility

It can be good to be underappreciated, to go unnoticed, to feel invisible. In our achievement-focused, award-based, trophy-giving world, it's difficult to appreciate the value of invisibility. Of course we want our work to be acknowledged and respected. Recognition and rewards keep us going, especially when the work is difficult and we've stuck with it through setbacks and adversity. And especially if we've achieved the results that were asked for. We want the world to notice us.

However, if we're engaged in doing things differently, in finding new ways to solve old problems, in discovering new methods and techniques, we have to expect to be invisible, even if our new approaches are very successful.

This dynamic is called "paradigm blindness." We all see the world through a particular lens, and we can't see anything beyond that. Anything new and different isn't visible. It's not that we personally are invisible—it's our way of being in the world that is.

If people *are* willing to notice our work, their lens will filter out what's new and different and only bring into focus those achievements or methods that look familiar. Everything else, all the innovative, bold, new things we've done, will be invisible.

People don't make a choice to ignore us—it's just that we all see the world through the lens we've crafted over many years of experiences and interpretations. Aspects of our lens are created by our culture, our parents, and by ourselves. To create a new lens takes work. We have to be committed to noticing our blind spots, and actively seek information that we didn't see at first. We have to notice what we're not noticing and commit to this practice as a discipline. But most people won't undertake this work. They'll continue to ignore us, and we'll continue to feel invisible.

Below the radar, if we don't need recognition, we can get a lot of good work done.

We're never gonna survive
unless we get a little bit crazy.

Seal
Singer/songwriter

Frustration

From time to time, it's good practice to surprise ourselves with new behaviors. Especially when our familiar techniques aren't working and we're frustrated. At such moments, most of us do more of the same. We act as if our approach is fine, it's just that we're not applying it correctly. So we become more focused, diligent, hard-working, frustrated.

When things aren't going well, when the results we need aren't materializing, it's time to be different. It's time to choose a new response. We don't have to choose a better response, it just has to be different.

Choosing a different behavior is risky. We're going to look strange to those who think they know us. But in many cases, they already think we're strange, so perhaps the risk is not as great as we fear.

We don't do things differently to upset people. Changing our behavior is how we discover we have choice. There's no reason we have to stay locked into how we've always done things. As soon as we break free of the prison of our habits and patterns, as soon as we take the risk of trying something different, freedom greets us.

Noticing our freedom is the essence of this practice. That's why it almost doesn't matter which new behavior we try out. Whatever we do that's different releases us from the familiar; any change introduces us to the space of possibilities rather than the confinement of habitual patterns.

Over time, of course, we want to discover responses that are appropriate, that better serve to accomplish our purpose. But these too will become overly familiar and eventually frustrate us.

Frustration is a guide to freedom, if we recognize its signals.

We can put our whole heart into whatever we do;
but if we freeze our attitude into for or against,
we're setting ourselves up for stress. Instead, we
could just go forward with curiosity, wondering
where this experiment will lead. This kind
of open-ended inquisitiveness captures the
spirit of enthusiasm, or heroic perseverance.

Pema Chödrön
Buddhist teacher

Experiments

Life is just one big experiment and so are all our efforts and great intentions to impact our world for good. If the solutions to problems—personal and global—were known, they wouldn't be problems now.

Even though this logic seems rather obvious, it's strange how so many people keep applying old methods and old thinking to these issues, even as they keep failing. It seems we'd rather keep exhausting ourselves with failure than change our minds and admit that new ideas are needed.

Truthfully, we don't have the faintest idea what to do.

Yet this is not an admission of defeat, it's an invitation to experiment.

Instead of exhausting ourselves with doing the same thing only faster and with more vehemence, we could shift into curiosity.

Curiosity is a very compelling space—open, rich, friendly. We're willing to be surprised rather than having to get it right. We're interested in others' perspectives, intrigued by differences, stimulated by new thoughts.

Curiosity is a very pleasant place to dwell. Relaxing even. And most certainly fruitful.

All it requires is letting go of certainty and admitting we don't know what we're doing.

Let the experiments begin.

Human life should be like a vow, dedicated to
uncovering the meaning of life. The meaning of
life is in fact not complicated; yet it is veiled
from us by the way we see our difficulties.
It takes the most patient practice to begin to see
through that, to discover that the sharp
rocks are truly jewels.

Joko Beck
Zen teacher

Clarity

It can take many years of being battered and bruised by events and people to discover clarity the other side of struggle. This clarity is not about how to win, but about how to be, how to withstand life's challenges, how to stay in the river.

We never learn to triumph over life, but we can learn that every defeat, every problem, every terror is a teacher that prepares us for the next hardship. And we learn to expect that there are always more difficulties ahead.

When this clarity emerges from our experience, what also emerges is trust in ourselves. We realize that we can cope and learn and grow from hardship and trials. We learn to accept difficulty and setback as part of life's normal processes. We cease feeling threatened by most things.

Instead of struggling or avoiding difficulties, we become people who know they can hold their ground even as the currents intensify and threaten to drag us under. We learn to sink our feet into the mud ever more deeply, because we know that more challenges are coming.

Once we've experienced life in all its dimensions—good, bad, hard, easy—life doesn't seem so challenging. Every situation is what it is, sometimes lovely, sometimes difficult. Every situation is workable.

We're fully in the river and we're learning how to keep our heads above water.

The essence of the false promise is that we can
make ourselves and our life whatever we want.
But this will only bring disappointment,
because no matter what we do, there's no way we can
guarantee a life free of problems.

Ezra Bahda
Zen teacher

Life Is Life

What is it about us humans that we think we need to control everything? Actually, this isn't true of all cultures—most indigenous people and traditional cultures participate with life, work with its unceasing cycles, and expect there to be good times and bad times.

But in Western culture, we believe we're smart enough to control everything, including Mother Nature. We certainly think we can control what happens in our own lives. If this weren't true, why would we be so obsessed with planning and goal-setting?

What would it feel like to surrender to the rhythms and dynamics of life? What would it feel like to realize that we don't really have a choice here—we can either participate with life, or resist it and drive ourselves to exhaustion and failure.

Instead of working so hard to actively construct our lives, we could relax with the opportunities that life provides, both the good and the bad ones. People who have this type of relationship with life truly are more relaxed. The seeming loss of control doesn't create anxiety or feelings of distress. It does the reverse, it creates feelings of ease and clarity—and the capacity to stay.

Surrendering to life offers some wonderful realizations. We learn we're capable of being in this dance, of working with whatever happens. We learn to trust ourselves and then others and, gradually, we learn that life itself can be trusted.

The grace of surrender offers us the awareness that life is on our side, that life is our partner. Whatever may be happening in our private worlds, inside the noise and disturbance, a lovely realization dawns.

Life wants us here.

Pleasure is not a reward.
Pain is not a punishment.
They're just ordinary occurrences.

Chögyam Trungpa
Buddhist teacher

Just Like Me

Anytime we're experiencing a dark emotion—grief, anger, fear, loneliness—we can be assured that all over the planet, millions if not billions of people are experiencing the same thing. This is true because we're all human. Even though our external experiences differ profoundly, our emotional responses are the same.

In the midst of overwhelming emotions, even a momentary recognition that we're having a shared experience can transform our experience from personal to communal. Even when we feel crushed by isolation, abandonment, loneliness, if we can flash for a brief instant on all the others who are in the same state, it changes our experience. Perhaps our awareness is short-lived, but even a few seconds is enough to recognize that we're not completely imprisoned by these emotions, that, in fact, we can use them to connect to others who are also suffering.

Once we experience this connection, our pain isn't quite so oppressive. We've taken a moment to look beyond our personal experience and that simple gesture of looking outside ourselves creates more space within us. There's a little more room for our hearts to open, to experience compassion, connection, even gratitude.

When we recognize that our personal struggle is fundamental to being human, that everyone struggles and suffers, we begin to feel less personally victimized. We become more accepting of difficulty, less battered by bad moments.

It takes but a moment to notice what's going on in the world beyond ourselves. At every instant, no matter what we're feeling, we always find ourselves in the very good company of hundreds of millions of people.

My continuing passion would be...to part a curtain,
that invisible shadow that falls between people,
the veil of indifference to each other's presence,
each other's wonder,
each other's human plight.

Eudora Welty
Writer

Clear Seeing

To want to see clearly is a true act of fearlessness. To open our heart and mind, to be open to what life is offering us in this moment, requires tremendous courage and steadfastness.

In the openness, we will encounter the information we pushed away, the messages we wouldn't hear, the ideas we rejected, the people we made invisible.

Our openness also invites in penetrating emotions—grief, sorrow, love, compassion.

We do not create the space of clear seeing with our usual methods. No questioning, no analysis, no distinctions—just bearing witness to what's present. The less we sort, judge, categorize or distinguish, the more we see and feel.

Without our usual filters and boundaries, we stop feeling repulsed or threatened or thrilled. We discover that we're much larger than our usual boundedness. In fact, we're big enough to take it all in.

And wonderfully true, the more open we become, the less fear is present. Fear does a very good job of keeping us from being present, filling us with thoughts about what might happen in the future, or what seemed to have happened in the past.

But in this present moment, fear is nowhere to be found. Clear seeing has no fear. We are in this very moment released from fear's mesmerizing grip.

To be free from fear, we merely need to be in the present moment. Then we can see clearly.

If we have been aware of the process of our lives,
including moments that we hate,
and are just aware of our hating—
"I don't want to do it, but I'll do it anyway"—
that very awareness is life itself.
When we stay with that awareness,
we don't have that reactive feeling about it;
we're just doing it.
Then for a second we begin to see,
"Oh, this is terrible—
and at the same time, it's really quite enjoyable."
We just keep going, preparing the ground. That's enough.

Joko Beck
Zen teacher

Success

What are your measures of success? Both your conscious ones that you proclaim, and your unconscious ones that manipulate you invisibly? When you get depressed or upset with yourself because you've failed, what measures are revealed by your distress?

At the end of your life, what measures of success do you expect you'll still be clinging to or proudly proclaiming?

Can you accept as a measure of success that you just kept showing up, day after day, even when you weren't feeling helpful or effective?

What about the times you didn't get caught in others' dramas, or weren't swept away by dark emotions?

Or the times you refrained from striking back and refused to counter aggression with aggression?

Or the moments when your heart opened to another person's predicament because you'd had the same experience and realized we're all just only human?

Simply staying on the path, no matter what, keeping on with your direction, finding your way back when you get lost or diverted—this seems enough success for a lifetime.

If we've returned again and again to our work, if we've taken on challenges rather than avoiding them, if we've known when to give up, when to change, when to open up, when to love...

Well I, for one, will feel very successful.

PART FIVE

For We Are the Ones

All that we do now must be done
in a sacred manner and in celebration.
For we are the ones we have been waiting for.

...in reality there's nothing anyone can
give us. There's nothing that we lack. Each
one of us is perfect and complete, lacking nothing...
But this truth must be realized by each one of us.
Great faith, great doubt, and great determination
are three essentials for that realization.

John Daidi Loori
Zen teacher

The Path

Great Doubt
Who am I?
Why am I here?
What's the point?
Why me?
How do I get out of this?

Great Faith
I'm here for a reason
I trust that I can learn and grow
I trust that other people are worth the struggle
I know that every situation is workable

Great Determination
I'm willing to keep going
I choose to stay
I surrender to what is

In the dark time, there is a tendency to veer
toward fainting over how much is wrong or
untended in the world. Do not focus on that.
There is a tendency too to fall into being weakened
by persevering on what is outside your reach,
by what cannot yet be. Do not focus there...

We are needed, that is all we can know.

Clarissa Pinkola Estes
Writer

Opening

Two opposing movements determine a great deal about our capacity—either we open or close, we withdraw or step forward, we turn toward or away, we look inward or outward.

It's very difficult to open and move beyond ourselves if the world is hostile and frightening. If we're being attacked, misrepresented or in danger, we instinctively seek to protect ourselves. Whatever armor we've developed quickly wraps around us. We may hide behind harsh words and gestures, we may disappear emotionally. Anything to defend ourselves. In such moments, opening to the world feels dangerous and downright suicidal.

But armor can't protect us for long. The more we protect ourselves, the less capacity we have. We can hunker down and develop stronger defenses, consumed by fear and aggression, but after doing this for a period of time, there won't be much left of us. We will have cannibalized ourselves.

Opening to the world gives us strength, the will and capacity to persevere in hostile environments. But this doesn't mean that we open ourselves foolishly, standing there like a target, accepting whatever people throw at us. This has been aptly named "idiot compassion."

What we do open to is the information and messages we've shut out. We open to the people who still need us even as a few are attacking us. We open to what our work is now in the face of opposition. We open to the realization that this situation is workable. We realize that we have to open, no matter how fearful it may seem.

Fear always dissolves as we face it directly, We can be assured that things will be less fearful once we open. In the brighter light of undefendedness, we'll be able to see the way forward.

If you're not on the edge,
you're taking up too much room.

Bumper sticker

Edge Walking

People who persevere walk the undulating edge between hope and fear, success and failure, praise and blame, love and anger.

This difficult path often feels razor sharp and dangerous, and it is. Scientists call it the edge of chaos. It's the border created by the meeting of two opposing states. Neither state is desirable. In fact each must be avoided, no matter how enticing or familiar it appears. Possibility only lives on the edge.

Security is not what creates life. Safety, safe havens, guarantees of security—none of these give life its capacities. Newness, creativity, imagination—these live on the edge. So does presence.

Presence is the only way to walk the edge of chaos. We have to be as nimble and awake as a high-wire artist, sensitive to the slightest shift of wind, circumstances, emotions. We may find this high-wire exhausting at first, but there comes a time when we rejoice in our skillfulness. We learn to know this edge, to keep our balance, and even dance a bit at incalculable heights.

Walking the edge never stops being dangerous. At any moment, when we're tired, overwhelmed, fed-up, sick, we can forget where we are and get ourselves in trouble. We can lapse into despair or anger. Or we can get so caught up in our own enthusiasm and passion that we lose any sense of perspective or timing, alienate friends, and crash in an exhausted mess.

The edge is where life happens. But let's notice where we are and not lose our balance.

Vigilance

Do not follow low practices.
Do not live carelessly.
Do not hold wrong views.
Do not prolong the suffering of the world.
Whoever moves from
carelessness to vigilance,
lights up the world
like the moon that emerges from a cloud.

The Dhammapada

I have no parents: I make the heavens and earth my parents.

I have no home: I make awareness my home.

I have no divine power: I make honesty my divine power.

I have no means: I make understanding my means.

I have no magic secrets: I make character my magic secret.

I have no miracles: I make right action my miracles.

I have no friends: I make my mind my friend.

I have no enemy: I make carelessness my enemy.

I have no armor: I make benevolence and righteousness my armor.

Samurai Warrior
14th century Japan

Groundedness

Do you know the ground you stand on? How well do you know its strengths, its pitfalls, the places that give you courage, the places where you get stuck? Do you know where to find your ground when things get bad? Do you pay it any attention when things are good?

Nobody gets through life ungrounded. But unless we know this and are conscious of the ground we stand on, we may be shocked to discover that what appeared as granite is, in fact, quicksand.

Ground has to be cultivated. We create ground by nurturing our convictions, by learning from our experience, by developing trust in ourselves and our world. These cultivation activities require hard work, as any farmer would happily warn us. We can't let our attention lapse, we can't just blindly push through our everyday lives and assume we're staying grounded. We're not—we have to take time to learn and reflect, stepping out of the fray to observe it periodically.

As much as we need to cultivate ground inside ourselves, we also need to be grounded in things beyond ourselves. This can be our faith, our love, our awareness. Whatever it is that calls us outside our narrow sense of self and invites us to participate in a world far more wondrous than any person can imagine.

Knowing our ground, and knowing it well, consciously attending to it and taking good care—this is the only way to withstand turbulence.

Even the most outrageous stream has a muddy bed that serves to keep it within bounds, enabling it to find its way to the sea.

I said to my soul, be still, and wait without hope
For hope would be hope for the wrong thing; wait without
    love
For love would be love of the wrong thing; there is yet faith
But the faith and the love and the hope are all in the waiting.

T. S. Eliot
Poet

Faith

The journey of perseverance begins with fire, with passion for our cause, with hope to change things.

As the journey continues, passion dissolves into weariness. The obstacles are larger than we expected. The insanity is more than we can bear. But still we travel on, one foot in front of the other.

And then there comes a point when we realize that we will not see our work bear fruit before we die. And that's o.k. We feel content that we have planted seeds for some future harvest. That we have met good people. That we have learned many things. That we have survived this far and lived to pass on the stories.

We're certainly not the first ones to have our dreams pushed so far into the future that we won't live to see them. Consider Moses or Abraham or Martin Luther King. They each carried clear visions revealed to them by their God, but they also knew they would not live to see these promises fulfilled.

What led them forward was faith, not hope. Faith in the truth of their visions that came from a source beyond petty needs for satisfaction and accomplishment.

Perhaps holding true to the vision and not losing our way is enough for one lifetime.

Abandon Success

Do not depend on the hope of results...
you may have to face the fact that your work
will be apparently worthless and even achieve
no result at all, if not perhaps results opposite
to what you expect. As you get used to this idea,
you start more and more to concentrate not on the
results, but on the value, the rightness,
the truth of the work itself...
gradually you struggle less and less
for an idea and more and more for specific people...
In the end, it is the reality of personal relationships
that saves everything.

Thomas Merton
Catholic monk, writer, activist

The reward of patience is patience.

St. Augustine, born 354

Patience

Perseverance is a journey seemingly without end.

Yet it has a few destinations or rewards, one of which is patience.

It's not that we start out patient. We don't persevere because we are patient people.

We become patient because we have to. There is no choice—the work is endless.

Everyday we have to make a choice. Will we give up, or will we keep going?

When day after day we are willing to keep going we discover, quite to our amazement, that we have become patient.

And then we just continue on. Day after day.

In my grief I saw myself being held,
us all holding one another in this
incredible web of loving kindness.
Grief and love in the same place.
I felt as if my heart would burst with holding it all.

A Zimbabwean woman

Joy

People who experience true horror in their lives, or those who befriend them during war or natural disaster, frequently recount that joy was part of their experience. For those who haven't been in these situations, the ability to feel joy in the midst of tragedy seems unimaginable. Perhaps they're just putting on a good face, glossing over their terrorizing experience, or in denial or repression. We feel so badly for what they've suffered that we don't let our sympathy be disturbed by the possibility that there also was human goodness in what they endured.

But joy is available in the worst, most dehumanizing situations. If we allow this fact, we can learn a great deal about our human spirits, about who we are.

Joy, like peace, resides only inside us. It is never manufactured by external circumstances. This is very good news, as external events, other people, and life in general become more harsh and difficult. But discovering what lives deep inside us, as our natural condition, requires fearless curiosity.

If we look deep into ourselves, what do we think we'll find? Dark emotions, scary desires, endless negativity, unstoppable fear? Or do we expect we'll discover joy? To investigate our interior, we have to trust that we're more than a collection of very bad things. We have to have faith that, at our core, we're essentially fine, whole, healthy. And we have to believe this about everyone, not just ourselves.

The potential for joy is always present in us but, like everything in life, that potential only becomes evident in relationship. We can't analyze whether joy exists, or hope to discover it from a remote, isolated position. We have to be together. We have to be in service to one another to discover our essential goodness.

This is why people can discover joy even in the most horrific situations. They were together.

Live to the point of tears.

Albert Camus

Fruition

Where does all our hard work get us? What's left when our work hasn't shown any tangible results, when we've failed to achieve anything noteworthy, when we've been disappointed by people, leaders, friends, ideals?

A life of discipline and awareness, where we've exercised choice, served others as best we could, learned as much as we could bear—such a life yields a very rich harvest. The fruits of our labors are not to be found in the world, however. They're inside us, in how we feel about self, the world, life, others.

If we rummage around inside ourselves, we might notice that there's less fear, more curiosity. We might notice that there's more space, that there's room for choice, that we now contain a larger repertoire of behaviors.

We probably will notice that our heart is enlarged and that, even though it takes up a lot more space and demands more attention, it holds good things. The giant emotions of anger, grief, loss, fear, now cohabit well together. There's enough room for all, and seldom does any one of them get out of hand. Our big hearts also produce a lot more courage. We've grown unafraid to open ourselves to the dilemmas of the world, and to work with them face-to-face.

Perhaps most surprising is our sense of comfort in the world. We've grown to feel we belong here, that life wants us here, that there are more than enough good people to be with and to struggle for.

We've lived fully, we've experienced joy, we've had some fun, and we'd do it all over again.

Lord,
There is a big devil called
Discouragement.
We ask you to send him away because he is bothering us.

Haitian prayer

The Five Strengths

Strong Determination

You continually reaffirm your strong longing to
continue with your work.
You are pleased to wake up in the morning and pleased
to go to bed at night.

Familiarization

You have developed your skillfulness.
You know what you're doing, your work is a natural
and familiar process.

Seed of Virtue

You have tremendous yearning to offer your work.
You do not feel that you've had enough of it or that you
have to do something else instead.

Reproach

You silence the inner voices of doubt, negativity,
self-loathing, ego.

Aspiration

You are willing to serve any worthy cause that helps
the rest of the world.

Adapted by M. Wheatley from Chögyam Trungpa
Buddhist teacher

Raven, Teach Me to Ride the Winds of Change

Perch where the wind comes at you full force.

Let it blow you apart till your feathers fly off and

you look like hell.

Then abandon yourself.

The wind is not your enemy.

Nothing in life is.

Go where wind takes you

higher   lower

backwards

The wind to carry you forward will find you

when you are ready.

When you can bear it.

Margaret Wheatley

Time to Play

A busy executive was speaking to her six year old niece at the end of a particularly frustrating day. She'd spent the better part of the day trying to get a new printer installed. Nothing had worked, and she was exhausted and very frustrated.

On the phone with her young niece, she described in general terms how frustrated she was.

Her niece asked, "Did you try hard?"

"Yes," she replied.

"Did you try really, really hard?"

"Yes I did."

"Well then," said the six year old, "now it's time to go out and play."

We Knew

Well we've known

we've known

we've had a choice

We chose rejoice.

Devendra Banhart
Singer/songwriter

About the Author

MARGARET (MEG) WHEATLEY, Ed.D.
writes, teaches, and speaks about how we can
organize and accomplish work in chaotic times,
sustain our relationships, and willingly step forward to serve. Since 1973, Meg has worked
with an unusually broad variety of organizations: her clients and audiences range from the
head of the US Army to twelve-year-old Girl Scouts, from CEOs and
government ministers to small-town ministers, from large universities
to rural aboriginal villages. All of these organizations and people wrestle
with a common dilemma—how to maintain their integrity, energy, and
focus as they cope with relentless upheavals and rapid shifts. But there
is another similarity: a common human desire to live together more har-
moniously, more humanely, so that more people may benefit.

Meg has written seven best-selling books: *So Far from Home: Lost and
Found in Our Brave New World*; *Walk Out Walk On: A Learning Journey
into Communities Daring to Live the Future Now* (with Deborah Frieze);
Perseverance; *Leadership and the New Science: Discovering Order in a
Chaotic World* (eighteen languages, third edition); *Turning to One Another:
Simple Conversations to Restore Hope to the Future* (seven languages, second edition); *Finding Our Way: Leadership for an Uncertain Time*; and *A
Simpler Way* (with Myron Kellner-Rogers). Her numerous articles appear
in both professional and popular journals. Her website,
www.margaretwheatley.com, contains a treasure trove of articles, pod-
casts, and video clips available for free download. Also available for pur-
chase are DVDs, conversation starter kits, and other products.

Meg has a doctorate in organizational behavior from Harvard University and a master's in media ecology from New York University. She also studied at the University of London. She has been a global citizen since her youth, serving in the Peace Corps in Korea in the 1960s, and has taught, consulted, or served in an advisory capacity on all continents (except Antarctica). She began her career as a public school teacher and has been a professor in two graduate management programs (Brigham Young University and Cambridge College).

She is cofounder and president of the Berkana Institute, founded in 1991. Berkana has been a leader in experimenting with new organizational forms based on a coherent theory of living systems. Berkana has worked in partnership with a rich diversity of people around the world who strengthen their communities by working with the wisdom and wealth already present in their people, traditions, and environment.

In 2003, the American Society for Training and Development honored her for her contribution "to workplace learning and development," dubbing her "a living legend." She was elected to the Leonardo da Vinci Society for the Study of Thinking in 2005 for her contribution to the field of systems thinking. In 2009, she was appointed by the White House and the Secretary of the Interior to the National Advisory Board of the National Parks System to support a 21st-century culture of adaptation and innovation throughout nearly 400 parks.

She returns from her frequent global travels to her home in the mountains of Utah and the true peace of wilderness. She has raised a large family, now dispersed throughout the United States, and is a very happy mother and grandmother.

About the Artists

ASANTE SALAAM is a galaxy of artistry born, raised and rooted in New Orleans. The stars already shining in her galaxy include sketcher, painter, mixed media collagist, artist's book maker, assemblage sculptor, writer and printmaker. As an artist, holistic wellness practitioner and life coach, Salaam aids people in pursuing dreams, taking informed risks, manifesting new realities, and adopting practices to live a juicier life.

Asante holds a BFA from the School of the Art Institute of Chicago. She has been featured in publications including Oprah Winfrey's "O" Magazine and is based in New Orleans. Asante and Meg met through a mutual colleague in post Katrina New Orleans. Communicating and working long-distance, Asante created the original paintings to illuminate Meg's writing and the Hopi prophecy. Asante's abundant artistry can be enjoyed at *www.AsanteSalaam.com*.

BARBARA BASH is a calligrapher, author, illustrator and performance artist living in the Hudson Valley of New York. Studying Dharma Art with Chögyam Trungpa and Chinese pictograms with Ed Young, she became interested in the joining of Western calligraphy with Eastern sensibility. During this time she began working with large brushes, exploring what makes a mark alive.

Barbara has written and illustrated a number of books, among them *Desert Giant: The World of the Saguaro Cactus; Urban Roosts: Where Birds Nest in the City; Shadows of Night: The Hidden World of a Little Brown Bat*. Her most recent book is *True Nature: An Illustrated Journal of Four Seasons in Solitude*, written out in her own hand. Barbara teaches expressive brush and illustrated journaling workshops throughout the US and Canada. Visit her website and visual blog at *www.barbarabash.com*.

References for citations, permissions and further information:
www.margaretwheatley.com/perseverance.html#references

Also by Margaret J. Wheatley

So Far From Home

Lost and Found in Our Brave New World

So Far from Home is best thought of as the "prequel" to *Perseverance*. It describes how, in spite of our best efforts to change this world to be more fair, just, sustainable, and enjoyable, we have ended up in a world no one wants, a harsh, destructive world that overwhelms and exhausts us. This book details how this world came into existence and encourages us not to withdraw from despair but to gladly take on a new role as warriors for the human spirit. Even with so much difficulty and darkness, we can still do meaningful work, using values we cherish and attending to the relationships and issues we care about. *Perseverance*, then, is the day-to-day manual for how we can stay in the middle of the river and be of service to others.

Paperback, 200 pages, ISBN 978-1-60994-536-7
PDF ebook, ISBN 978-1-60994-537-4

BK Berrett–Koehler Publishers, Inc.
www.bkconnection.com   **1 800 929 2929**